Jesus and Me Every Day

Eira Reeves

Book 1

Published 2009 by CWR, Waverley Abbey House, Waverley Lane, Farnham, Surrey GU9 8EP, UK.
Registered Charity No. 294387. Registered Limited Company No. 1990308.

For a list of our National Distributors, visit www.cwr.org.uk

Concept development, editing, design and production by CWR

Printed in Latvia by Yeomans Press

ISBN: 978-1-85345-518-6

CONTENTS

Many, many years ago there was only darkness. But God wanted to do something very special and create a beautiful world out of the darkness.

Talkabout How do you feel when it's dark?

Prayer Dear God, please be with me when it's dark so that I'm not scared. Amen

First, God shone light into the world and it became very bright and brilliant!
God was delighted with what He saw because now there was day and night.

Talkabout When it's dark and you switch a light on, what happens?

Prayer Dear God, thank You for light so we can see.
Amen

Then God decided to make a sky and it looked wonderful! He wanted everyone to enjoy how different the sky can be each day. God was very pleased with it all.

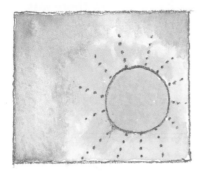 

 Can you point to the picture that is like the sky today and talk about it?

Prayer Thank You, God, for the very beautiful big sky You made. Amen

Next, God wanted lots and lots and lots of water in the world. He also made land. The water swished and swirled around the land. It was all very exciting!

Talkabout What do you like about water? What can water be used for?

Prayer Dear God, thank You for all the ways we can use water. Amen

God then planted loads of plants, trees and flowers. All of them made the world look very colourful and bright. God's beautiful world was beginning to take shape.

Talkabout Can you point to your favourite colour in the picture? What colour is it?

Prayer Thank You, God, for vegetables, flowers and trees for us to enjoy. Amen

Guess what God made next? Loads of birds, fishes and animals, spiders and butterflies, elephants and sheep and much more! God smiled at everything He had made.

Talkabout 'In awe' means amazed. Say what you are in awe of in God's world.

Prayer Thank You, dear God, You are so clever making all of these! Amen

But God wanted something much more special. So He then created two people and called them Adam and Eve.
God even made a garden for them because they were His friends.

Talkabout God wants friends to love. Are you His friend?

 **Prayer** Dear God, help me to always be Your friend. Amen

Genesis 3 verses 1–7

God trusted Adam and Eve and He talked to them often. However, one day Adam and Eve were very, very naughty. They disobeyed God.

Talkabout Have you seen someone who has been naughty? What did they do?

Prayer Please God, would You help me to be good today. Amen

God was very sad about Adam and Eve and they had to leave the garden He had made for them. Adam and Eve knew they had been naughty.

 **Talkabout**

What makes you sad? Can you talk about it?

Prayer

Dear God, I know I can talk to You when I am sad for I know You will be with me. Amen

Because Adam and Eve had been naughty they had brought trouble into God's beautiful world.
From then onwards God's world was spoilt.

Talkabout

What do you think of Adam and Eve?

Prayer

Dear God, I am sad that Adam and Eve made You sad. Amen

A long time after God had made the world He had another special plan for the world. Mary, who was going to marry Joseph, lived in Nazareth.

One day an angel, called Gabriel, had a message for Mary.

Talkabout

Talk about how you like God's special plans.

Prayer

Dear God, thank You that You have a special plan for me. Amen

Luke 1 verses 46–55

Angel Gabriel told Mary that she was going to have a very important baby. They were to call Him Jesus.
After hearing this message Mary sang a song praising God.

Talkabout

Can you sing a song praising God? Perhaps you can make one up.

Prayer

Thank You, dear God, we can sing to You when we are sad or happy. Amen

Some months went by and Mary and her husband went on a long journey to Bethlehem. When they arrived there wasn't any room for them to stay and they had to sleep in a stable.

Talkabout

What do you think it was like to stay in a stable?

Prayer

Dear God, thank You for finding a place for Mary and Joseph to stay. Amen

Luke 2 verse 7

During the night, the very important baby was born to Mary and Joseph. They called Him Jesus. Mary carefully wrapped Jesus up and placed Him in a manger.

Talkabout Do you know anyone who has just had a baby? What was so special about the baby?

Prayer Dear God, thank You that You knew about me before I was born. Amen

Luke 2 verse 16

Not far from the stable where Jesus was born were shepherds looking after sheep. Angels appeared to them. 'Quick,' they said, 'go and look for Jesus.'

Talkabout

What would you have felt if you were with the shepherds?

Prayer

Dear Jesus, I just want to be like the shepherds and look for You. Amen

Matthew 2 verses 9–10

Some time later, after Jesus was born, three kings saw a big star in the sky. They knew that a special King had been born. So they travelled some distance to find Jesus.

Talkabout Do you like going on long journeys? What do you do as you travel along?

Prayer Thank You, dear Jesus, for the three kings who travelled a long way to find You. Amen

Matthew 2 verse 11

The three kings found Jesus and they gave Him gifts. Then they bowed down and worshipped Him. Mary and Joseph rejoiced because they knew that God was the Father of Jesus.

Talkabout

What gifts do you like giving friends?

Prayer

Dear God, thank You for Your gift of Jesus to us. Amen

Everyone was playing together. Kim boasted that he had given his best toy to David. Sue very quietly gave her favourite toy to Sarah.

'Thank you,' said Sarah.

Talkabout

Which way of giving would Jesus prefer?

Prayer

Dear Jesus, when I give something away help me to do it quietly Your way. Amen

Give what you can

'Great, thanks Daddy," said Sue when he had given her some pocket money. With some of the money Sue bought a present for her mummy.

This made her mummy very happy.

 **Talkabout**

Are you given pocket money? What do you like to do with it?

Prayer

Dear Jesus, thank You that You give to me so that I may give to others. Amen

Always when Max goes to church he puts some of his pocket money into the church collection.
Max knows that Jesus is pleased with this because he's helping other people.

Talkabout

Jesus helped poor people. How would you like to help them?

Prayer

Dear Jesus, show me how I can give to people who don't have much. Amen

When you give something, Jesus loves it if you give from your heart. But most of all He loves it if you do it with both a happy face and a happy heart.

 **Talkabout**

Can you say ways that you give with a happy face and a happy heart?

Prayer

Dear Jesus, please help me to give happily to You and others. Amen

Noah was a very good man and he loved God and God loved Noah.

Now God had a very special plan for Noah and God trusted him to follow His plan.

 Talkabout

Say ways that you want God to trust you.

 Prayer

Thank You, God, that You trusted Noah. Help me so that I can be trusted by You too. Amen

God said that He was going to flood the earth because the people had disobeyed Him. So God asked Noah to build a HUGE BIG boat!

God wanted to save Noah!

Talkabout What do you think Noah thought of God's plan?

Prayer Thank You, God, that You had already worked out this plan for Noah. Amen

Building the boat

So, just as God told him to do, Noah built a BIG, BIG boat. He sawed wood, chiselled and banged nails until the boat was finished. It was HUGE!

Talkabout — What do you think Noah's family thought when they saw the boat?

Prayer — Dear God, help me to listen to You just as Noah did. Amen

Then God told Noah to put two of every animal onto the boat. There was a lot of squealing, roaring and squeaking from the animals as they climbed onto the boat.

 **Talkabout**

What noise of an animal can you make?

 **Prayer**

Thank You, God, that all the animals and Noah and his family were safely on the boat. Amen

Then it began to pour with rain and the boat floated away. The rain just poured and poured down. It was such stormy weather, but Noah was safe on the boat.

Talkabout

What do you like about a storm? What don't you like about a storm?

Prayer

Dear God, help me when I am frightened of a storm. Amen

Some while later the rain stopped.
Noah knew it was safe for the animals
to leave the boat.
Noah was very happy and so were all
the animals!

 What is your favourite animal and why?

 Thank You, God, for keeping Noah safe. I
know You will keep me safe too. Amen

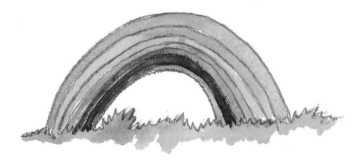

To show Noah that He would keep His promise and never flood the earth again. God made a rainbow in the sky. God wanted to bless Noah.

How does God bless you?

Prayer

Thank You, dear God, for all the blessings You give me and my family. Amen

Matthew 18 verses 1–3

Jesus loves children

Jesus loved to be with little children, and children loved to be with Him. Jesus always wanted to protect children because they were precious to Him.

Talkabout

Wherever you are, do you think Jesus goes with you, and why?

Prayer

Thank You Jesus, I know You are with me all the time. Amen

One day, the friends of Jesus asked, 'Who is the greatest in the kingdom?'
Perhaps they were hoping it might be one of them!

Talkabout
This 'kingdom' means a place where Jesus is.
Would you like to be in this place and why?

Prayer
Dear Jesus, I always want to be in Your kingdom. Amen

Jesus looked around Him and saw a small child. He called him over and stood him in the middle of His friends.
The friends wondered what Jesus was about to say.

 **Talkabout**

What are the good things about being small?

Prayer

Dear Jesus, it doesn't matter to You that I am small, You still love me very much, thank You. Amen

Jesus explained to His friends that in their hearts they should become like little children ... then they will be with Him in His kingdom.

 **Talkabout**

What do you think Jesus' friends thought when He said this to them?

Prayer

Dear Jesus, thank You that You want us all to be like little children and trust You. Amen

Jesus told His friends that whoever welcomes children would welcome Him too.
Little children were very important and special to Jesus.
They still are!

 **Talkabout**

How are you special to Jesus?

Prayer

Dear Jesus, thank You for always welcoming me with open arms. Amen

Matthew 19 verses 13–14

Lots of mummies and daddies brought their children and babies to Jesus.

'Please bless my child,' said one mother. Then a mummy and daddy asked, 'Please pray for our children.'

Talkabout

Who do you like praying with? Can you say why?

Prayer

Lord Jesus, I pray that You will bless my family and me. Amen

There was a shepherd who looked after sheep. His name was David and his home was in a small village called Bethlehem. David had seven brothers.

Talkabout

Can you say how a shepherd looks after his sheep?

Prayer

Thank You, dear Jesus, that You are my shepherd and keep me from harm. Amen

David took care of many sheep on faraway hills during the day and night. He played a harp and sang songs whilst he was alone.

Talkabout Would you like to play an instrument? Can you say which one?

Prayer Dear Jesus, I want to sing and praise You like the shepherd David. Amen

One day David took some food to his brothers because they were in an army and fighting. One of the enemies was a very BIG giant called Goliath. Everyone was so scared of him!

 **Talkabout** Is there anything you are scared of? Tell God and He will understand.

Prayer Dear God, help me when I'm scared and help me to be brave. Amen

'I'll fight that BIG giant Goliath,' said David to his brothers.
'I know I can beat him.' David said this because he trusted God.
But one brother was angry with David.

Talkabout — What do you think David's brothers thought?

Prayer — Dear God, help me to trust You in everything
I do. Amen

Goliath found it very funny that someone soooo small as the shepherd David should fight someone like him who was soooo BIG. The giant laughed and laughed.

Talkabout — Has anyone made fun of you or laughed at you? Can you talk to someone about it?

Prayer — Dear God, help me to share how I feel. Thank You for helping me. Amen

David put a stone in his sling and aimed it at Goliath the giant.
WOOOOOSH. Suddenly the BIG giant keeled over and died.
David had won the battle!

 Why was David brave? Look at Day 38 again.

 Dear God, thank You for David's courage and trust in You. Amen

God had special plans for David, the shepherd, because He loved him. It was sometime later God told David, 'I'm going to make you King of Israel.'

What a wonderful plan of God!

Talkabout Can you say why God loved David? Do you think God has plans for you?

Prayer Thank You, God, for helping David the shepherd to become a king. Amen

A HUGE PICNIC

John 6 verses 2–5

Feeding time

A HUGE crowd had gathered by a lake and they were listening to Jesus teach.
Then Jesus said to His friends, 'Everyone is hungry here, what shall we give them to eat?'

Talkabout Have you been on a picnic recently? Where did you go?

 Thank You, dear Jesus, that You teach us such a lot. You love us to have picnics too! Amen

'Feed this lot!' cried out Philip one of Jesus' friends, 'but how can we? We don't have enough money to buy food for this HUGE crowd.'

 **Talkabout**

Can you remember a party you've been to? How many people came?

Prayer

Dear Jesus, thank You that it's not a problem for You when You want to feed lots and lots of people. Amen

Just a small portion

Then Andrew, another friend of Jesus,
found a little boy who was willing
to give his food away.
But it wasn't very much,
just five loaves and two
small fishes!

What meal would you give a friend if they
were hungry?

Thank You, dear Jesus, for the little boy who
gave his food away. Amen

'OH NO!' said all of the friends of Jesus. 'This food will never ever feed a huge crowd.'
But Jesus had other ideas. He knew He could feed the crowd with such a small amount of food.

Talkabout

Do you believe Jesus could feed the crowd? Why?

Prayer

Thank You, Jesus, that we can trust You whatever You do. Amen

'Sit down,' said Jesus to the crowd. Then Jesus lifted up the basket of two fishes and five loaves and said grace. Everyone was waiting to be fed.

Grace is saying thank you to God for food. Do you ever say grace before a meal? What do you say?

Prayer Dear God, thank You for all the food You give us. Amen

The basket of five loaves and two fishes was handed around the huge crowd. Everyone was fed from this small meal. After the crowd had eaten they were all full!

 What do you like to eat when you go on a picnic?

Prayer Thank You, dear Jesus, that we can feel full after a meal. Amen

Do you know what, even after the huge crowd had eaten the meal of five loaves and two fishes, there was some food left over. Everyone in the crowd was so amazed.

Talkabout This is called a miracle. Tell about times you have been amazed and why.

Prayer Dear Jesus, You love to amaze us. Thank You. Amen

Mummy was in the kitchen. 'Can I help?' said Ben. 'I want to make a cake.' So Mummy let Ben stir the spoon in the bowl of the cake mixture.
'Well done!' She said, encouraging him.

 **Talkabout**

Who do you like to help and why?

Prayer

Dear Jesus, help me to help others. Amen

Sarah loved to paint and draw. 'I know,' said Mummy, 'why don't you paint a picture for Kelly. She's not feeling very well at the moment.' Sarah enjoyed painting a picture for Kelly.

To Kelly ...
Jesus loves you

Talkabout

Can you draw a picture of Jesus for someone today?

Prayer

Thank You, Jesus, for giving me fun when I draw and paint. Amen

It's a special day today and David and Kelly are helping their playschool teacher, Mrs Brown, to arrange the chairs.
All the grown-ups were going to visit!
'I like doing this,' said David.

Talkabout

What is your favourite job helping others?

Prayer

Dear Jesus, let me always offer to help others. Amen

'Mrs Brown is in hospital,' said Mummy to Kim and Kelly. 'Let's go and visit her.' On the way they bought some grapes for her to eat. 'Thank you,' said Mrs Brown.

Talkabout

If someone was ill what would you like to do for them?

Prayer

Dear Jesus, when someone needs help show me what to do. Amen

Naughty people

'Go to Nineveh, Jonah,' said God. 'I want you to tell the people of Nineveh to behave themselves and stop being so very naughty.'

Jonah wasn't sure he wanted to go to Nineveh.

Talkabout

Do you think you or other people you know are naughty sometimes? Can you remember when?

Prayer

Dear God, help me not to say or do naughty things. Amen

'No God,' said Jonah,
'I'm not going to
Nineveh because I don't like the people there.' After he had
told God this Jonah ran off in the opposite direction.

Talkabout
What do you think of Jonah not obeying God?

Prayer
Dear God, help me to obey You when You ask
me to do something. Amen

Jonah ran and got on a boat with some other people. He felt all right because he wasn't going to Nineveh now and he was so glad.
But God sent a storm.

 **Talkabout**

Have you ever done the opposite of what you have been told to do? What happened?

Prayer

Dear God, if I have been naughty, I am so sorry, please forgive me. Amen

'I'm so sorry,'
wailed Jonah,
'it's all my fault there's a
storm. You see I've disobeyed God.'
So the people on the boat decided to throw
Jonah overboard. Poor Jonah.

Talkabout

If Jonah had done what he was asked, do you think he would have been in such a mess?

Prayer

Please, dear God, help me to listen and do what You tell me to do. Amen

When Jonah was thrown from the boat, the storm stopped. As Jonah swam, a BIG fish swallowed him up. For three days and nights Jonah was in the fish's tummy.

Talkabout
Can you talk about what it must have been like in the fish's tummy?

Prayer
Dear God, when strange things happen in my life, help me to trust You. Amen

Inside the fish's tummy, Jonah swirled around in the dark and cold. He felt awful and didn't know what to do. So he prayed for God's help.

 **Talkabout**

Have you ever prayed for God's help? What happened?

 **Prayer**

Dear God, when things aren't going right, please help me. Amen

Out of the BIG fish

All of a sudden the fish spat Jonah out! What a surprise answer to prayer. Jonah flew through the air and landed on the beach. He was so exhausted.

 Have you ever been surprised when a prayer has been answered? When?

Prayer Dear God, thank You that You listen to our prayers and answer them. Amen

Jonah obeyed

On the beach, God told Jonah again to go to the people of Nineveh who were naughty and speak to them.
This time Jonah obeyed God and the naughty people became good.

Talkabout
If someone was naughty, could you speak to a grown-up about it?

Prayer
Dear God, help me to have courage sometimes and speak up. Amen

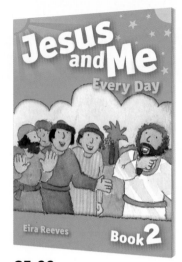

£5.99
ISBN: 978-1-85345-519-3

Sixty more beautifully illustrated daily devotionals by Eira Reeves, for 3- to 6-year-olds:

- Young Jesus
- A special job
- Love
- Moses, a great leader
- A man who cared
- Peace
- Elisha helps
- A little man
- Praising and thanks
- Abraham

For when you're too old for Jesus and Me Every Day

Topz helps 7- to 11-year-olds get to know God and His Word through an exciting, day-by-day look at the Bible. Daily Bible readings and simple prayers are augmented by readers' contributions along with fun and colourful word games, puzzles and cartoons.

£13.80 UK annual subscription (6 issues)
Individual copies also available: £2.49 each
72-page, full-colour booklet, 210x148mm, published bimonthly
ISSN: 0967-1307

Visit **www.cwr.org.uk** or call **01252 784710**
Prices correct at time of printing.